NASCENT ILLUSION

NATHAN HASSALL

Copyright

ISBN number: 978-1-4477-8622-1

Acknowledgments

I would like to give a special thanks to those who have helped me produce this book. Firstly, I would like to thank Linda Lovett for her kind assistance and considerable time spent formatting this book. I also thank John Speed who designed the front and back covers. My final thank you goes to my mother, Sharon Hassall, for her assistance with proof reading and editing.

Dedication

This book is dedicated to my Grandmother, Shirley Anderson, who passed away on 07/02/2003, age 83.

Contents

SHORT STORIES

6th July 1998—
Cutting the Grass Party

Mother described such an undesirable situation to me the other day. She started off with that serious tone she uses that Father used to call bitch tone. I always laughed when I heard Father say bitch tone because it did not make sense to call another human being a dog, so the irrationality in Father's comments struck up a laughter chord within me. The difference was that Mother did not like it and she used to get really angry about it. She said my queer grinning was uncalled encouragement for Father to keep winding her up, like a toy. Anyway, she started moaning about the lawnmower and how she poured diesel into it, even though she should have poured petrol into it. I told her to use petrol carefully because it can ignite and create all sorts of problems including third degree burns. I am sure she took a mental note of this because she paused and rolled her eyes, which clearly showed that she could see what I meant. She went on to say that she had no idea how to get it fixed and that Frank from down the street was not in. This was significant because Frank is a handyman and normally provides services to Mother for free. Sometimes I did not like it when Frank came round. He always used to try and talk to me and high five me and I had absolutely no idea why because usually I high five for something that I enjoy and I did not enjoy him. Basically, going back to Mother on the lawnmower, she was bitterly disappointed that she could not cut the grass for the party tonight. I offered that I go outside and ingest the grass so that it looked like the lawnmower was used. She politely declined this offer and told me that I was stupid for wanting to do that. But in all, the day was okay and the party went well. The guests started off being quiet and after a long time they were really loud and making barely any sense. I correlated their change in behaviour per millilitre of alcoholic liquid that entered their systems. Jan and Damien, Mother's two best friends from school, are staying in the spare bedroom next door to me and they are bumping around a lot. There are still loud and noisy people outside, playing with all the long grass Mother wanted to cut. I know this will make her rather bemused. I started to get really annoyed at all the noise going on so I went to the room that Jan and Damien were in to issue them an instruction of silence. As I walked in, I saw not Damien, but Frank bounce on the bed and then freeze. I told him I was surprised to see him. I looked around and saw Mother. She looked hot and bothered. As I walked towards her, she told me to stop. Straight after that, Frank pulled scissors out and held them to Mother's throat. He told me that he would not cut Mother, if I promised not to scream.

08th December 1998— 4.56pm—Birthday

I do not really understand this concept of 'birthday.' Do you celebrate the fact that you have lived for another year? It does not sound like something you should be congratulated for. People have done much more impressive things like splitting an atom, we don't celebrate January 3rd every year so why this? Mother says it's a traditional ritual that is prominent in many cultures. Father says it's an excuse for Mother to drink alcohol. I had some alcohol once that I took from Mother's cupboard. The bottle had a name; it was called 'PORT.' I consumed this and then everything was blurry and I spat acidic liquid out of my mouth. It also had some bits in it. I do not understand the point in consuming liquid if it is just going to come out again. It contradicts the body's needs for fluids. Stupid illogical body. I hated the feeling of dizziness this morning. Lots of Mother's talking felt really loud and it was as if a man was running around my head with a mallet banging my skull. I knew there was not a man there though, as he would not fit in my head unless he was some sort of really small man, who got a specially made really small hammer from 'D.I.Y Dan's' down the road. I always found D.I.Y to be rude. Imagine if they did it in a restaurant, if I went to Giles and ordered ham egg and chips and the man in the Giles uniform just said 'do it yourself,' it would make me feel angry and sad because the primary function of the restaurant is to cook you food, providing you have sufficient funds to pay for it. On my birthday the big Giles uniform man brought out a cake with candles on it. What a waste of candles because I did not care that it was my birthday and I do not really like cake. Maybe in Africa they would have wanted it instead of it being wasted on me. Mother always says that in Africa there are people who are poor and starving. I think it's similar to when I get up late and miss breakfast Mother cooks for me. Then I am hungry until lunch. For breakfast I usually get two eggs and two rashers of bacon in a sandwich. However, on my birthday, I got some sausages as well. I liked to watch her cook it and I especially liked when the oil in the pan spat at her. Last time it happened, she let out a high pitched, "Ouch!" and it was really amusing but it only hurt her temporarily, which is nice, because I would not really want Mother to be hurt and especially not on my birthday. Anyway, the cake I had was the first one I got to blow the candles out myself but I did not want to blow them out as I was bemused by the dancing fire on the candle heads. Maybe they also knew that it was my birthday and therefore celebrated by doing a birthday dance. I did not want to blow them out because it really smells once the fire stops and I did not want to displease my nostrils. The small fires the candles created inspired me. I told Mother this and she replied, "don't say such stupid things." I was not saying stupid things, because I was not lying. It really did inspire me and that's why I wrote it all down. When Mother uses that tone of voice Father calls her a cow. Cows are used for beef. It is dinner time so I must go and eat now. I will switch off my story brain and engage in conversations with Mother. I shall discuss my discussions shortly.

30th December 1998—
Final Memories

I remember how satisfied I used to be when watching water boil in a kettle. I used to glare at it with contained enthusiasm. Watching steam escape from its surroundings used to cause elation within me. How ecstatic liquid water seemed to be when it changed forms. I still dream about learning how to change. Sometimes, I used to turn the kettle on with barely any water in it. It gave the machine short satisfaction in its quest and it made me chuckle! The microwave offered a bit of competition to a kettle in the sense that it was used to heat up various other liquids. For example, Mother used to heat tomato soup in a bowl. This created washing up though, much to the distress of the sink. I liked to turn the taps on and watch water flow freely.

"Stop wasting water," Mother would say. I hated being told that I was wasting water. I thought it was the cloud people that wasted water; they always chucked loads off their balconies. When too much was wasted, outside looked like a stream. I never made inside look like a stream, therefore I never wasted water. It was harsh of other people to cast those accusations upon me as there were worse things that used to happen.

I remember once when the red trucks turned up and the uniformed people made Mrs. Gren's bricks all wet. They told me it was because there was an irritated blaze flicking itself all over the place. Why if the house was not living did the uniformed people water it? I always got told that living things needed water and that is why I gave my hamster Harold a bath. He did not move for hours. After Mother came in from work she looked worried but she took him out for a drive. When she came back he was full of life. His fur had even changed colour! From then on I was no longer allowed to bath Harold.

Water, I did not realise then, could also be evil. I regret submerging myself in this lake. Relaxation followed by suffocation and back to relaxation. I get it now. I hope Harold is where I am going. Then, I may have a chance to see him with the cloud people, and fulfil mothers wish by getting them to stop wasting water.

Sharpest Tool in the Gut

Circles are shapes which have infinite sides. I have always found this to be impossible to imagine. The laws of infinity seem to confuse even the sharpest of us. Circles are sometimes sharp, and they are continuous curves. Knives are sharp but are equally confusing. Why use the letter 'K' in knife if it is to be silent? It is absolutely ludicrous and unforgiveable. The thought process behind such silence is illogical and action must be taken.

What is it with numbers and letters? Why are they at war with each other? Ha! Numbers and letters fighting is daunting. However, I have always wondered about the victor. I was thinking of doing a survey in town today to see what other people thought on this matter. The Alphanum war regularly makes me scream.

Ahhhh.

Apparently I'm not allowed outside today.

Selfish prick.

They say I'm not the sharpest tool in the box, but I have one.

YOU KEEP QUIET. Always shouting at me. Fucking letters.

I have a plan. Being number 3423556 can always be inspiring.

Letters understand the door locks; they are the providers, the givers of food. The circular ticker meets in a descending vertical manner when the provider comes along.

It is time.

It is quiet until the door opens.

Good evening, Officer K.

Maybe that's why the K is silent in knife. As your red victim shuts up.

You cunt. Don't call me a maniac.

Distressed Chess

I was teaching this girl to play chess today. She was in a large empty room with a potent echo. It was similar to a school sports hall. If you were to shout, you would hear a voice respond with the same words, albeit quieter. Basically, I told this girl a few things about the chess pieces:

Pawn—an admirable piece, willing to protect the monarchy in the game but only useful in numbers. From working class backgrounds, they are blinded into helping the nation for the 'greater good' (to protect the interests of the rich). She asked why the game had black and white pieces and if it showed segregation between black and white cultures. I responded no, they were just two opposing colours. I went on to teach her the rest.

Rook—often misconceived and called a castle. The two bastions crafted by gifted architects. Movable only in straight lines, if only life was that simple! The girl was rather inquisitional, asking how the castle moved at all. I explained to her that it was a game and therefore metaphorical. She nodded and I believe she understood. I think she was getting the hang of it.

Knight—the nobles, rich, great fighters, Lords. All male of course. The only non patriarchal piece on the board was the Queen; even so the King was still the most important piece.

Bishop—monarchy, a piece that Marxists and anarchists would not enjoy. They offer only a diagonal route which is a stressful scenario when a piece stands intimidatingly in front of it. The girl was annoyed at the illogical nature of this piece. I told her more.

Queen—Self explanatory. But she can move anywhere. She is there to protect the King, taking women's usually domesticated issues onto the battlefield to strike down opponents. Being less important than the King shows the perhaps harsh social hierarchy.

King—Need I say more? Fat, lazy, lumpy, slow. He cannot move more than one space and he needs protecting. The girl asked why he was so important and no-one else. I gave her a lecture on the divine right of kings, how they are important because they use the excuse of God, their belief that women are below them. She did not like this, and neither did I.

Obviously, I explained the rules further, I spoke about check and check mate and she seemed to be at peace with the game. However, much to my distress, she refused to play the game. Smart move I thought, even though chess is enjoyable, I would easily beat her! I did try and play chess with her once but she could not touch the pieces.

The girl stared at me in a cold blooded manner. I felt uneasy as she started to sob. I asked her what the matter was. She gave me this response:

"I am dead."

Of course she was, stupid me. Obviously she could touch the pieces if she was alive!

I wish I had a living friend to play chess with; it took me ages to learn the rules.

Fighting Mother Nature

I am so angry at Mother Nature. She keeps making annoying things happen to me. If that dissatisfied wind keeps blowing around I'm going to slap a fucking tree in the branch. I will also proceed to construct a massive ladder into the sky and rip the fabrics out of the clouds. I will make this ladder with wood used from deforestation, which will show her. If she wants to displease me, I'll smash her creation. I'll pull leaves off of trees; pull grass out of the ground. I'll burn soil and murder wildlife. My car will be left on so that CO_2 emissions can rise into the air. If she wants to attack her ponds with acidic rain just to try and get me, it'll be her problem. This personal battle must be fought. Women cannot have such power, their minds are unstable. I want to take over and call it Father Nature. People will know and worship me. Yes, I'll be the King of Nature. I'll affect people's lives in ways they didn't know was possible. Oops! My mistake, that spider is now dead. Look at him, pressed against the bottom of my shoe. It's only a matter of time until she gives in, I hope. Stupid stubborn bitch.

Sadistic Doctor

Here are a few life lessons I believe everyone should know, in this guide that everyone should care about.

I am a wizard, my magical capabilities stretch far beyond the medicinal. I will wave that magic wand and you will believe pretty much anything I want you to. I prescribe you God awful people with whatever I want and you will believe that it will make you better, without even conducting your own research! I will give you the green light for drugs, to contrast with your hideous spotty red face.

Side effects? Well, maybe a few. A change in hormones, dry mouth, urinary retention, blurred vision, constipation, sedation, sleep disruption, weight gain, headache, nausea, diarrhoea, abdominal pain, loss of libido, agitation, anxiety... but that does not matter, it NEVER happens to anyone! Believe in my magical knowledge and it could do you the world of good. If certain effects were to kick in (and I am sure they will not) quit the real medication and I can shove some placebo up your arse. I can put you under the knife, hack at you like a mower cuts grass. It is all for your benefit. Remember, I wear a uniform; it is obvious that I want to help you.

I laugh at you poor idiots that walk in, grotty jeans, ripped shirts and shoes that are falling apart. There is a cure for that too! I call the disease "pooritisacalisc disorder"—rich people cannot get it, although we are the only ones that understand it.

Feeling queasy? Well lie down on my chair, I will stick a used syringe in your arm to sort out the sickness.

I hope you did not tell anyone of this private appointment, because I wish to conduct my experiment on you. It is whether the less fortunate have organs that are inferior to mine. I just have to stop your heart for an extended period of time, so say your goodbyes!

Thank you for listening, feeling tired?

Dr. F. U. Rat

Circular Communications with a Singular Spinner

I washed someone else's sock today. I watched it spin on a slow cycle on 30 degrees. It was a fantastic experience. It spun and spun and spun and spun. The sock would get to the top of the metal inside the washer and fall back down to the bottom. I really enjoyed the repetitiveness. Just for a treat, I turned on my fan as well. That had similar spinning characteristics. An excellent accompany to the washing machine.

As rotation is something like, I put a clock in the same room. Tick tock, tick tock, tick tock, tick tock. It had a comfortable reoccurring sound. I started spinning to it all and made myself dizzy, which caused me to fall on the floor and crack my head.

My rotations were evil and reminded me how dangerous patterns can be. This is why I stopped wearing chequered shirts.

I apologise.

I hope they know to come and get me. I cannot wait for the sirens to get me off my back and pull me out of this floor. Ha, I forgot about the disco ball on the ceiling.

What a ridiculous room I live in.

Time Kills and Flies

I know the secret to time travel.

I turned three times anti clockwise in order to protest towards the clocks conventional movements. I reversed time terminology by muttering tock tick instead of tick tock. I knew this was one of the puzzles to the overall picture of time. It was 11.11 when I started turning and the clock still states 11.11, so I must have gone back to yesterday morning. That means I'm late for work! Shit. My boss will not be too pleased. I'm altering and changing things I probably shouldn't be messing with. At least one with a stable mind is the only person that holds the metaphorical key to this unconventional way of travelling. Now I can reverse my mistakes of later as I'm fully aware of what situations to avoid in order not to have 'the accident.'

Maybe I should have gone to the future to see the consequences of my actions today. The problem is I wouldn't want to upset my twin brother with alternative aging patterns. The twin's paradox would create raging jealousy within him. You know what? Fuck work today, I could always go back in time again and go to work then. I'm going to treat myself to something nice. I could kill someone! It wouldn't matter, because I can go back in time again and then they would be alive again. I have always wondered what it would feel like. Would it be wrong? I mean they are not really dying because I will go back in time again and they will be alive, I think. Unless the universe is dimensional and every situation and outcome has happened somewhere because dimensions are infinite. I enjoy questioning ethical issues. Let us see what happens.

Everything is still dark. That's odd. I thought I went back to the morning but maybe it's yesterday evening. It's odd living in today when it's actually yesterday. It's like when they say tomorrow never comes, it always becomes 'today.' Hmmmm. Let's take a wander.

Everything is eerily similar in the past. The neighbours' cars are outside and parked exactly the same. Oh wait, where is John's car?! It was definitely here yesterday. Maybe I've changed the course of History and he no longer exists. I'm definitely panicking at this.

I've glanced around for a while. Staring at sign posts and wondering which route I should take. I feel sorry for sign posts, they give you directions and you never do anything in return for them. This inspired me to apologise for the countless times I have not thanked this particular one, which I'm going to name Percy. Percy has served many people greatly in the past and will do so in the future. I thanked him and gave him a satisfying pat on the post as I carried on my way towards the town centre.

I need to search for the ultimate victim. Male is always good. I'm not sure it matters; I will reassure the terrified faces that they won't actually die, it'll be a sort of illusion and they will not even be aware of it when time goes back to normal. Unless I create a time warp and that person dies constantly at the same time on the same day everyday. What an interesting concept for me to think about for a short amount of time. Okay enough of that, I'm wasting time. Or am I? I have an infinite amount of time because I know the secrets of stopping it as well. That means I'm immortal. Maybe I have certain divine qualities. There is a reason God gave me the knowledge of this and no one else. Thank you, God.

Okay. So now that I talked about my divine capabilities and they have been theoretically proven by me, I have not only the ability, but the right to end things which are not mine. But only things I think are bad. I will do it on my gut instinct; my digestive judgements are flawless. I liken it to a television program. If I do not like what's on, I would turn it off. If I do not like a person, I'll turn them off. The remote is the weapon for the televisions mind, like a blade is a weapon to a human's heart. I'm very humane; I do think televisions need to be treated fairly. I am an electronic protestor and I've seen what people do to old televisions. This pisses me off.

What makes his movements so robotic? This is the past not the future. He should know this. Maybe I should query his actions. I shall swat this fly in front of me first. They see time in slow motion but I can't speak their language so it would be difficult to ask them the secret of slowing it down. If you don't get something and know you can't, get rid of it so it stops confusing you. ARGH! This one got away. I need to gain my composure. I think it's time to go fly—swatting. A trip to the local 24/7 is necessary for this particular quest. I can go onto bigger and better things thereafter. What an exciting night in 'store' for me. Ah, my love for puns made me really want to do that! Shopping time.

The guy behind the counter looks suspicious. He has untrustworthy eyes. Maybe he knows I'm from the future. "I am from the world of tomorrow!" I violently shout towards him. His eyes divert and now he looks awkward. Maybe I should stop staring but his fear is amusing to me. Time to purchase that fly swatter. Out I go...

Now I have to go and find this fly, or one of his friends, or a member of his family. I'll teach them not to share their knowledge of time! Maybe this is a dangerous thing for me to do. I do not tell of my time travelling knowledge so maybe someone wants to swat me.

I should be careful, my swatter is yellow and yellow has always been the wrong colour for me. This is because I got stung by a wasp when I was younger, but at least wasps move in normal time. I used to catch them and put them in the freezer. Their stillness was hilarious! I really need to stop these procrastinating thoughts, it's getting stupid. Now with my weapon of choice I'm going to hunt flies and make them drop. I will tell them that time 'flies' when you're having fun. Their time will halt and they will drop to the floor. Bastards! I'll have the last laugh.

I have found the place of congregation. A terrifically terrified group of flies. Shame I don't have a wingman to distract some whilst I play the game of death with the others. Actually I wouldn't want that, I work alone. All alone. Ooh, is that buzzing I hear? I'll take my... ugh... mighty sweep and...HA! Got the cheeky fucker. Let that be a lesson to all of you flies.

"Not quick enough for me are you?" Maybe I have mastered it. I managed to get one. I should bring it home for autopsy. Or I could eat it and inherit its powers. I'll put it in my pocket for now and continue. I have something sharper for this next game.

Sorry, my friend, you have been spotted. You useless piece of shit. That's a rather tasty looking alleyway I'm sure you'll agree. Your footsteps are crystal clear and in high definition. The sounds you let off impress me but you are creating this unwanted feeling of sadness.

You look like me?! But how...? Maybe this is my past self but I don't remember walking through here, not ever. Let's end this... There is only enough room for one of me so you're going to have to take your punishment like a man. My blade is withdrawn. I'M RIGHT BEHIND YOU! There we go... sshhhh. No woman is attracted to a man that screams. Remember how they used to call you *twinny one*? Well, I'm number one now. Our parents wouldn't have approved but, hey, they used to give you all of their time...

Yes, I knew the secret to time travel.

The Ambient Chronicles:
Bus Sex Monologue (1)

I stepped up into the beautiful machine. I had a premonition three seconds ago that I was going to be asked for one pound forty.

"One pound forty that is," the man said. So I gave him one pound fifty to which he explained, "no change, get in my fucking death trap." I clambered on, bewildered. I could have been forgiven for thinking I was getting on a bus. I felt utterly perplexed.

"Next stop, go and fuck yourself," the intercom erotically suggested. I asked this lady where we were going. The spherical hag in front of me explained that I could get off at any destination printed on the route map above my head. She further elaborated with a point of her wonky index finger. I ridiculously obliged and then I asked the hag why she reeked of elephants' excrements. Presumably in response to this, she lustfully raised her handbag and caressed it upon my complex face.

"You would not want me to go off" I said, winking. I caught someone's eye.

"Fuck off to whence you came, you tramp," a triangular figure bellowed.

Not really understanding which realm I was in today, the ride came to an abrupt halt. I gleefully made haste. I went into an off-licence to purchase some essentials—vodka and cigarettes and condoms and fruity polo's. This seemed to fuel the shopkeeper's happiness, evident by his ever present grin.

"An ugly fuck like you is never meeting a lady," he said.

"Thank you, you fucking lovely man," I replied, reaching in to kiss him on the cheek. For some reason his fist responded in a delicate clash with my face. "Stop trying to seduce me, sex pest," I exclaimed, swiftly exiting.

I wondered where to go next, realising that the local park was adjacent and full of wooden seateries. Scratching my bollacks, I proceeded. There were wonderful sounds of screaming sirens as people were recognising my celebrity status.

"That's him!" an old man cried. Before I knew it, I was involved in some sort of wrestling act with a sweaty blur of yellow. "Are you trying to sting me, like some giant frisky wasp?" I inquired. Realising that my hands were freely stuck behind my back, the man picked me up and escorted me to my second vehicle of the day. "Were you the one playing those lovely sounds?" I asked.

"Shut up, weirdo," he gasped sensually. I was in fantastic dismay, especially impressed with the way the interior was put together. The wire metal stopped me from being able to lick the wasp man in the face.

"Buzzy day?" I spoke. Relishing his response, I leaked some sort of white liquid. "Ahhh," I said as I continued the free flowing climax. "I seem to have dampened the seat," I repressed.

The trip seemed to end softly.

26

The rest of the journey escapes my memory really.

The Ambient Chronicles: Kidney Science Fighting Reality (2)

The short queue in front of me has the interesting stench of boredom. Low life pointless specimens are waiting for their tests, interested in the long term financial gain. I am different though, a man of science, but I refrain from wearing the stained white jackets. The door in front of me creaked open.

"Next in," said the man. I grunted whilst deciding to pluck a hair from the inner part of my left ear.

"I will keep this one for examination later," I whispered, intentionally spitting on the man in front of me. There was no response, not even the slightest of twitches.

"Next in," the voice droned for the first time again. The spit man followed. Knowing I was next, the growing elation of anticipation surrounded my very being. I peered to my left. A young girl was stuck to the purple ceiling, she muttered the words:

"I was aborted." She followed up this bold claim with the deafening echo of laughter. This brought a salty tear to my eye, which descended into my mouth. I tasted it to find out its PH levels.

"An uplifting PH. Probably in the lightest shade of grey, with an essence of elderflower," I spoke to my cassette player.

"Next in," the slanted scientist groaned, standing at only two foot tall. I thought I would squash him like one would squash a mushroom but I realised this type of behaviour was inhumane and would go against the ethics of my study.

I approached this room and was confronted by three men; they had identical faces and were drooling at the prospect of me carrying out my tests on them.

"Lie down here please," they all said, expressionlessly and simultaneously. I climbed onto the bed and they grabbed each of my limbs and viciously stapled them to the mattress. They sat the bed up and nodded me towards the television. A film rolled in such beautiful colours, blacks, whites, various greys and a hint of electricity, to get my abstract attentions surging.

"Where are my manners?" I started. "I am from the planet Kartentine, much like the planet you are on, but the dimensions are different."

Their eyes widened. "Are you going to allow me to carry on my research?" I asked in a polite shriek.

The men left the room in a jolty fashion.

For obvious reasons, the television exploded. It oozed the most relaxing toxins. The calming scent battered my inner nostrils. One man came back into the room.

"We knew you would be here, organ donation is more effective from a person who demonstrates a fiery personality." He said. I was at the pinnacle of my happiness. A smile invaded my otherwise perfect face. I gazed at him in amazement.

"Try and take my kidneys first, they are a blasted pain," I revealed. I was starting to feel quite aggrieved as a silence forced its way into my eardrums. It was as if the silence was repetitively saying:

"I terminate your contract, I terminate you." The man walked out of the room again. Three green creatures bled out of the walls.

"Ah," I said. "Fellow scientists." They got closer to me; skipping out sequences that most people would need in order to travel. The green men started plugging all sorts of holes in my body; they were creating new ones and expanding on the originals. The young girl from before appeared at the foot of my bed.

"Ah, Timothy Traitor, you annoying little minx," I told her.

"Why are you trying to abort my twin? Without your kidneys you will not be able to take your grandmother out this evening. She does not associate herself with the kidneyless." I thought that was well put into a structured sentence, yet irrelevant. My grandmother is not due to be born for another four days and that is weeks before I give birth to my favourite portrait. I decided to sleep for awhile but my dreams were interrupted with my own voice instructing me to get off the bed.

"Drink this," a delicious glass of paint suggested. I did so, so I guess that was the end of my trip. My hypothesis was flawless: forty seven holes seemed to be a good way to extract my kidneys. Now I can fill the bottomless pit at the end of my garden with new found knowledge...

The Ambient Chronicles: the Power of Sin (3)

This is an odd room that I find myself in, one that does not resemble any other I know. There are statues of people kneeling with their hands clasped together; their eyes and lips are firmly shut. I approach the carpet through the middle of the hall, whilst taking time to look around at the dark drapes waving amongst the grand, triangular windows. There are three men at the front, all muttering words of prayer in a modest manner. They stop and look straight at me, all with singular eyes consisting of a stunning array of colours. Their blinks are contracted rhythmically. The man on the left goes first. As his eye shuts, the middle man starts to blink. As the middle man is halfway through the blink, the man on the right's eye starts. After repeating this four times, they turn 180 degrees and gaze towards the back of the room. They raise their hands and create circular movements, as if they are caressing a spherical object. Loud whispers crack around the room as the statues start shuffling.

"Step out of existence...," they say in unnerving collaboration. I accept and take one step to the left and begin falling down a hole as if into an abyss. The more I fall, the darker the pit becomes. Objects are starting to fly around me. The object that sticks out most is a grandfather clock with a melted face, groaning at the repetitiveness of its journey. The pendulum is only swinging from the middle to the right, hitting an invisible wall as it attempts to swing to the left. Thousands of daggers start pouring out everywhere; they come menacingly towards me until they hit me.

They bounce off me though, like light would reflect off a mirror. When the daggers get into the distance, they turn into stars and planets. I see somewhere to land so I fall softly onto a dusty landscape.

"We were expecting you," a young lady spoke, pointing me towards a house in a screaming explosion of colours. I attempted to move towards it but my feet were stuck in the ground.

"Well if you are going to be like that, I guess I will have to come to you," the house said whilst blinking its blinds in a disappointed manner. In a deafening screech, it dragged its way towards me. "Enter," it instructed. The door opened, inside was black. I entered without caution and found myself in the same queer looking room that I was in before. The door creaked shut behind me and the three men with giant eyes watched me once again. They started projecting images on the floor, images of wars in plain black and white. Footage of famine, despair, loss, grievance and general pain were flashing before me. I felt the familiar pain of battles once fought.

"What have you done to yourself?" a stern voice bellowed, it echoed around me. I walked back towards the three men again as they turned once more.

"Step out of existence…," they instructed once again. This time I ignored them and got on my hands and knees. I crawled towards them.

"The one with variable odours, why do you come back to us?" the middle man asked. I opened my mouth but all that came out was thick, grey cement. "You are impure, why do you stain our temple?" Two more men suddenly appeared, one on the right of them, one on the left.

"He is at fault for all our sins," the one on the right spoke, hauntingly, "but I will grant you with the power of imprisonment, so you are forgotten through the realms of the paradox." I nodded, against my will. "Do you believe?" he asked. I nodded once more. The statues raised and fixed their attentions onto me, with icy glares and unforgiving expressions.

"Step out of existence, you blasphemous objector," they shouted. A force crashed into me and sent me to the left. I felt myself falling once again, this time through a bright light. A cage surrounded me. I watched all my hopes and dreams, loved ones and aspirations gradually disappear. With that, the comforting light increasingly became blinding darkness. With this all my fears and phobias became all encompassing, they surrounded me. The cage was removed and my demons swiftly moved in to play with me. I was pushed and pulled, insulted and degraded. I felt increasingly weak and unable to put up any resistance. The torment was on an unprecedented scale, the grandfather clock reappeared and each ticking second was ever slower. The pendulum stopped working, it stayed on the right. Bells deafened me, cracks of thunder were lighting up the terrifying experience. I begged and begged and begged. I promised to join. I promised to believe.

"Step back into existence…" The familiar voices repeated. I appeared back in the room, this time on the same platform with the one eyed men.

"Convert," one instructed. I fell to the ground, shaking and twitching. I could smell acceptance and comfort. "You stay here with us," another went. "You have sold your soul." With that I lost all but one feeling, all my anger, sadness, happiness, jealously and affection had left me. As I stood up, my voice was back.

"I want everything, all the power and all the money possible," I said in a monotone voice.

"Yes… you are the sixth piece to the seven sins of our existence. With one more being, we can control everything." I touched my face. All I could feel was one eye.

"He is one of us," they all spoke, as our systems became dormant. We were all stuck; no-one was breathing, speaking or moving. We had to wait for one more in order to gain the control we so utterly desire…

An Erratic Notion

An erratic notion, one would have thought, two may have been different though. This game of numbers I was playing was of great amusement to the fellows that insisted on portraying their proud flags outside of my living room window. I rose to the occasion by presenting them with the most inviting choice of finger, one that people like to use when showing their non-verbal displeasure to a situation. Their response was careful, the wind rippled through their clothes as they used their intuitive thinking to cast their eyes of hatred onto me. There was a tense stand off. My body started growing until my head hit the ceiling. My muscles started pulsing. I punched through a wall and went outside. I glared down at the people I had sworn at. They failed to cower. They started climbing up my leg, hanging onto the hairs of my feet and shins as I grew ever taller, my head bursting through the clouds. The rain was obviously no longer falling on my head and all I could see was the sun's blinding rays. My body stopped growing but the length of my neck continued to increase. I could feel myself getting closer and closer to the moon. Eventually, I managed to rest my chin on it.

Fake the Reality of Real

I like to pretend things are fake.

I like to get fake things and pretend they are real.

My imagination is fake, my actions are real.

I act fake to make my imagination real.

WHAT < KCUF EHT > "Sir, the wordings are backwards!" I invoke.

I speak in riddles to aid you.

I hope you do not feel the pain, of which I am insane.
I wrote this poem for you, it's called bitter love.

START OF POEM ONE

I was only bitter
Because
You are one of those people
That I despise
You stupid bitch.

END OF POEM ONE

Not very poetic I guess, but at least I can get across what I was thinking through the art of literature.

Stop screaming, I have one more.

START OF POEM TWO

It is a loving blade
So I will give it to you

And take it away
I am afraid

END OF POEM TWO

Did you like that one?

No?

Sorry.

Now imagine I didn't stab you, that it was all fake and I will pretend that I wasn't here.

See you!

With loving condolences

Timmy

Hanging Outside

It's an idea to portray the contemporary events. There are ones and twos and sevens and nines... But I bet that's not important to you... No?

"Another classic again played at the theatre!" I remember this ridiculous voice bellowing. What theatre...? I was outside in the cold, living in a sleeping bag. Its exterior was red and black, its interior smelt of urine. It used to be the only thing that kept me warm; it reminded me of the bed I used to sleep in. I remember the hugs my mum used to give me for warmth, now I hug myself for comfort. My only friends are salty globules of water that descend down my face. My facial hair regularly catches my friends as they pass each other on the cheek.

I used to think about the homeless people when I passed them whilst walking through the subway, I used to call them tramps. There was an element of injustice in there, like walking through an art gallery of someone else's nightmare. I always wanted to get out of there, I used to be terrified. The trickling water and the crocking of pipes attacked the drums of my ears with violent rhythms. The men would groan and grunt, much to my discomfort. I am now sure that they were less comfortable than I was.

My interesting life takes another turn as I look for a new bed to keep me warm at night.

Mummy,

All I wanted was a hug.

Cheap Laughs

It was ecstasy. No other word for it, it was ecstasy; adrenaline fuelled my body with intense hostility.

I had broken through the barrier in my mind that previously stopped me from having the ultimate sensation. Finally, limbo had been overcome.

Having the ability to take what isn't yours but the inability to put it back again.

It could be argued that what goes around comes around, but I know that's not true. Everybody knows that I control the truth, no one else.

I don't find it fun anymore but the barrier in my mind has been breached, there is no turning back. It's not as glamorous as it was made out to be, but I guess that is down to my own clouded judgements.

I want to escape from this place now and go somewhere else.

The comedown is the worst part, it reminds you that your euphoric state has ended, therefore you have some digging to do, or so to speak. At least you only need one tool; the territory is perfect for its use.

Oh dear, we all know the papers would love to talk about this. I don't understand, why would a game treat its player so badly? Surely it would be easier if inanimate objects could dissolve at the touch of a button. There is no button though, well I couldn't find it. I guess the 'big man upstairs' did not invent one for this game.

No fucking reset so I cannot start over. It angers me but it beats the robotic motions of those living in 'reality.' Who needs money anyway?

I get my highs for free. That's what power does to you. Even ants know I am powerful. I choose which ones to pity and which ones to sacrifice.

I love to play God.

I see jealousy in other people's eyes and jealousy is a sin.

It seems my session is coming to a close as I'm bored now. At least he's under a bed of flowers, jealous bastard.

No they are not weeds, they are flowers...

Needle, Bench, Tramp, Drink

A memory crossed my mind the other day. I remembered this time I had pins and needles as I was lying down on a bench, a day where my fist pushed softly into my own face. I remember how numb my hand was, the strange feeling that pulsated from my hand down to my arm, the pins were jumping and the needles were piercing. I likened them to a virus spreading. That thought sparked an earlier memory of the peanut butter sandwich I had for lunch that very same day, very sticky!

I'm not sure it was appreciated that I'd occupied this particular bench, even worse so I'd littered it with the most delightful of green cans. I can remember saying, "Fear not good citizens, I shall clean up these cans. I use green as an indication of my care for the environment." Now I realise how stupid that sounds, as my green cans had red writing on them, which makes people think of evil, hell and death. Also, I do not know why I bothered speaking; I hardly got the attention of the abundance of the flies and ants, the latter of which had surrounded my kneecaps. What a silly fucker I can be! I should have said "excuse me" but they were working so hard I didn't want to be a distraction!

The pins and needles then entered my shoulders; they were cool, harsh and tingling. I decided to store that information in my brain, so I could think about it later. I did not think for too long, as I did not want my ego to grow.

Enough about me anyway! That was just one day on a bench.

I hate the cold sometimes, the loneliness. At least the green cans were my friends but I threw them away.

Sorry, I have the tendency to go off track, where was I? Oh yeah, pins and needles. They ended up everywhere, I felt weak and sick to my stomach. The beautiful familiarity that I was going to forget my suffering for a few hours was prevalent as I fell into a deep slumber.

Strangely, this all happened yesterday, now I am in an uncomfortable bed being fed through a tube.

Fucking hell, life can be fascinating. I really don't know why I told you this story, I have better ones, I just forget most of them.

Feud with the Glowing Glass

There is a scream released when the light is switched on. The extended period spent in darkness made the change in light viciously attack my pupils. My face is now clenched hard with a hand that feels almost identical to the one in my pocket. This is all very confusing and disorientating. The bulb thinks it has a victory over me, hence its gloating glow. It makes me jealous and just between me and this wall, slightly raging inside. The rage cannot be shown, as fair sportsmanship should be promoted and the bulb (however much I hate to admit it) deserves its fine victory. I can stand underneath him and give a fascinating impression to others that I have a good idea. So even though we are enemies in competition, we can work together to make an amusing spectacle. This would be pleasing, like sharing wine with someone you raced against.

Standing under the light satisfied me far less than I predicted. My hypothesis was far out, which is frustrating, I didn't look like I had a good idea.

I know how to end this feud. I could turn the gloating sod off! He is still there though, I'm far too aware of that.

I can still see in the dark, I eat my carrots. Maybe he can't see me when he's off, he doesn't eat. Maybe he's sleeping or hibernating.

I know, I'll creep up on him. Slowly does it, tip toe... Almost in touching distance and here we go... Oh look! You are all over the floor now. I forced you into a million pieces. Who is the victor? You don't look so

NATHAN HASSALL—SHORT STORIES

bright now… You won a battle, but I have won the war.

Strange Order

Thinking thought of thoughts was on the agenda in my meeting today. I was surrounded by people in suits, white shirts and long black ties. They were conversing about a particular investment that didn't go their way. I attempted to have an input but they shot me down with ignorance and stunned silence.

A new marketing ploy was part of the meeting's minutes.

I started to think about food, which included a thought process about all the different flavours I wanted to have dancing on my tongue and tantalising my taste-buds. With this thought, my stomach let out a rather crude rumble. It was trying to communicate with me; I did not know how to speak its language, so I started caressing it to see if it wanted a massage. I coupled this action with a slight groan, which disappointed the debating folk around me. Untrustworthy looks glanced into my general direction; I pointed a finger towards my unsettled stomach. They did not seem to understand, as they ignored me once more. One man had a piece of paper in his right hand and a pen in his left. He was writing on another piece of paper that was on his desk, frantically forming letters with unnerving accuracy. I realised that they were ordering a takeaway and got involved.

Cooking up Sadness

There was a time I used to watch how my father cooked for us. I liked to watch him, as he would always tell me life stories during the process. I remember this scorching Tuesday in the middle of July, with not a cloud in the sky, as father was cooking our usual dinner. There was a family of eight to feed, so he had much work on his hands. He would juggle his paperwork in one hand, a spatula in the other. What he worked for outside provided the food in the house, what he worked for inside got the food on the table. I remember to this day my sister Kelly outside, attempting to get a tan. Father would always remind her that sun could cause skin cancer and she would usually shout back at him. But not today, today was a sad day. I looked down at the tiles on the floor, sobbing quietly to myself. I watched my tears drop down.

There was a time I used to watch Mother cook, before she left us in a car accident.

Crash and Burn

Today is the day to make new friendships. Let them be peculiar, different to the 'normal' ones that people usually make. I will journey into the non-existent mind of the inanimate. To the minds that you take for granted, yet feel an emotional connection to.

I will start by flicking on my bedside lamp; allow it to glare at me with its single bulb. I will push it high so it can share its light with the ceiling. I will put cardboard cut-outs that I made earlier so that shapes appear above me, I will move them closer to the light and then further away. Their shadows will look as if they can grow and shrink, like a person.

Onto the admiration of the plug socket. There are two next to each other but only one is used, it's old and worn. The other is seemingly new, but appears lonely. I shall change them today; even the socket needs companionship. I smile at it but get the same three eyed woeful stare I'm very much used to. He could at least make an effort as I've matched him with my stereo plug. I thought that the socket would like being matched up with electronics, it would give him extrinsic satisfaction in knowing my ears are suitably satisfied with the beautiful chimes pulsating out of his friend, the speakers.

I think my bed has had enough, she looks suicidal. I'll help her; I've told her many times that I can be a euthanasia clinic.

I decided to set her alight, I did so and gleefully watched the flickering fire dance around.

It took a while, but the door was making loud knocking noises. I told him to piss off; he was getting on my nerves. I climbed under my desk and evaluated the situation.

The hot plague jumped around the room, onto the curtains, destroying the sad face smeared on my clothes.

With the last satisfying sip of my coffee, I attempted to sleep.

That's the last memory I have.

The floating feeling I have is in strange contrast to the burning one I felt prior.

I didn't know that I did so well, apparently I am on my third degree.

I didn't crash, but I'm certainly burning.

Delusional Belief System

People always seem to lose contact with their friends but I always stay in touch. If reality perceives these friendships to be false then there is a systematic flaw. You may not agree but these people are close to me. They are unshared and not for you.

I get told my sentences can be peculiar. Some describe my speech as 'word-salad.' Erratic and illogical people do not seem to understand that salad is healthy; therefore word-salad is a positive trait. How delusional of them.

Here is another term that gets thrown at me: episodic. Why is this? The people I see and speak to everyday are not part of a television series. They are real, ongoing relationships. Everyone else is too ignorant to acknowledge them. Others go as far as pretending they're not even in the room.

I hate how everyone has it in for me. I am made to meet this man twice a week who sits behind a desk. He always tells me that I will be okay. I don't get why other people wouldn't. Does no one else recognise the obvious?

People are too involved in their alter-reality and false importance of material success to think. 'Don't take drugs.' What an ironic thing to say. You lose friends from it. The funny thing is, the doctor told me to take drugs, to make me normal and healthy.

I'm pleased you listened. Most people ignore me when I tell them about my life.

It's kind of like... where did you go?

A Day to Remember
is Another Day I Forgot

The ice stands tall serving its primary purpose. I suppose the ice supports the substance of escapism. It slowly infuses itself with my last one of the day.

The inevitable time is near, the bell is almost rung. Sarcastic drones are soon to fill the air with predictable voice patterns.

The reasons people congregate here vary but the result of the trip is the same for all. The lifelessness of the place is evident, ironic for somewhere so busy.

The owner casts his judgemental eye with an underlying grin of satisfaction. Profiting from the depressed and the less fortunate.

The prison will open its door soon, yet we will never feel free. We are told we can leave whenever we want, but our minds know we cannot. Dependency keeps us here. Traumatic experiences bring us together but the different worlds we live in keep us apart. It will all happen again tomorrow.

There it comes. That soul-shattering noise. Eleven o'clock, we must finish. We had our last chance but we didn't take it. Maybe life needs to give us another chance. The last sip is as sweet as it is painful.

The illegal drive awaits.

The sound of death fills the air once the key is turned.

The ability to control has been hindered.

The challenge is there, away from the establishment I go.

I roll the window down, the policeman stands tall. 'There to serve and protect.' I usually get served a drink to protect my repressions.

This experience was different, yet inevitable. Splurging with slurs my logic was backwards. My recollection weakened, guilt surrounded me.

I awoke with new backgrounds, my outer prison had changed but my inner prison has enclosed even more.

In the slow destruction of my life, I managed to end someone else's. The worst thing is, I don't even remember doing it.

Hell Bound

It only takes a moment.

Why try to ignore the confusion that crosses your mind?

The door between reality and fantasy opens and the imagination influences perception.

It would have been easier if that word was not used; the hatred for that word fuels the raged mind.

The staircase should be blamed for taking part in such events; it seems unfair that all the focus is on one innocent character.

I blame him; the one that she believes built her. People believe in his existence, these people are confused.

At the bottom of the staircase there is a fire. Yet the heat is not felt and the flickering colours are not seen.

She doesn't know the fire is there, due to the sufficiency of her organ which consists of rhythmic contractions.

That one word slowed the rhythm; she will wish she never used it.

One word significantly decreased her death clock.

Only a matter of time now, the rhythm has stopped.

Time to wave goodbye, she has discovered the inferno.

It must be asked... where is her God now?

Search my Brain

Basically, in a stuttered way...

Suggestion one

He wanted to search my brain, so I offered that he climbed into my ear with a small flashlight.

Funnily enough, he did not fit, so we are searching for a different method.

Suggestion two

I attempt to extract my brain through my nasal passage, I was stopped during the act and received a lecture on why sharp objects are dangerous.

New methods must be searched. We must look to the illustrious sciences.

Fuck off science, I am a man of my word.

The silent silence scientifically and seductively whispered sentimental sayings straight into my non rhythmic ear drum.

You sent me here because I am mental? How stupid of you.

You are tone deaf and colour blind.

Where was I?

Brain food. Food for thought. I.

Suggestion three

I took my eyes out and stood in front of a mirror to see into my brain. I then realised that I could not see my brain, because I had no eyes.

I no longer saw what I was looking for in the first place, so I stopped.

Suggestion four

Curiosity killed the cat, it also took my fucking eyes out.

Conclusion

You need eyes to see.

Lonely Fishing

I go fishing alone sometimes.

I go fishing to cast away my dirty thoughts, impure thoughts. Get out of my head please! I am polite to my thoughts, even though I think they are fucking twats.

Allow me to vocally jazz my thoughts into your eyesight so that you can understand what I am feeling.

BRAIN WAVE OF DEPRESSION.

Has it smashed you in the lower pit of your stomach like a tonne of feathers? We all know they are the same weight as a tonne of bricks...

My inspiration is oozing out of me. Thick, black sludge is forcing its way out of my mouth; it is growing and turning into a fountain of infinite colours, pretty.

→ :)

YAY! But bad words lead to bad thoughts.

I think I should go fishing again.

Stupid fucking fish.

Confusion Pass

I had a test today:

If the square value of a water based creature rested itself on a rock would it:

A) Be unaware of its existence
B) Be aware that it is unaware of its existence
C) Be unaware that it is aware of its existence
D) Be existing unaware that it was aware of being unaware of existing

Naturally I circled 'D,' we all know the saying: "If four and three are A and B and C, stop being a prick and go and pick D." Our teacher used to tell us that one at school. He had quite the imagination. I remember when he used to teach "Thoughtology" – a subject which required only your own thoughts, and your answers could never be wrong.

Naturally, I got 100% in my exams and my parents showered me with gifts. I got a machete for my second exam and was advised to cut the hands of "The Establishment" off. Maybe I should have taken their advice seriously, as The Establishment then made sure I had my left hand taken off.

They did this because I knew too much.

It took me fucking ages to type this report without the use of two hands. I got asked to supply the class with my favourite words, the twist was that I had to use existing words and attach personalised meanings to them.

1. TWAT – a friendly businessman that looks towards the wellbeing of the consumer rather than to personal capital gain.

2. IRONY – the act in which something directly affects something else, like turning on a kettle to boil excrements.

3. CONFUSED – a four legged automobile that cannot move as it has no limbs.

I got so much appreciation for that! I will have to be off; as I have another Thoughtology lesson early tomorrow morning.

I will leave you with this:

If you travel back in time and meet yourself, but you only travel back one second into the past to exactly the same position where you were standing at the initiation of travel, what happens to yourself?

Your two beings will collide and cause an implosion.

I know, I am always right.

POETRY

Hurting our World's Minds

This is where we search for the answer
To the unanswerable question
This is where we
Attempt to uncover the truth of our existence

False presumptions of what we will find
Shell shocked, the end result is wrong in our minds
It will not make sense
We will realise divinity goes further than just
Breaching a clouded fence
Ticking time bombs clatter to try and make sense
Of something not understood
In this forest where all light is dense

We will always think about what we could have done
We know we could have reached the edge and
Cracked the mental cage
Stayed stable on the ledge
With a higher emotion
That falls deeper than rage
We are wasting our time
Something we have little of
This is something we fail to see

Our efforts in vain
Our nightmare sealed in propane
A colourless toxin we cannot view
The feeling of interior pain

Intrinsic emotions target us
They confuse us into unnecessary anger, jealously
and lust
What we tried to find

When uncovering the truth to mankind
Was welcoming, purpose and salvation

Instead
We see a destructed world
A reminder of our capabilities
Our notions of hatred
Our unwilling selfishness
Our greedy inflictions
On our fellow man.

Cannot Deal Alone

It's that kind of raw evening
Where you sit alone
Going over memories
Smiling over the distance

That kind of evening
You sit in your rocking chair
Thunder and rain bellow outside
Nature's instruments
Provide your only company

The reminiscent times
You hold your last love close to you
The metallic feel
Cold and harsh
Reminds you of hardship
Cries of what you could have done

On this evening
You look down
As you always felt
At the end of the day

So you take your only love
And face its only eye
With shaking hesitance
With knowledge of what you will commit
You get the courage
And pull hard with that one finger
All you catch is a glimpse
And then...

Nothing.

Housing all our Fears

It is inevitable
Impossible to see
The withering away of being
Remains taboo to society

Subconsciously it gets brushed under the carpet
Where the deepest thoughts of man lay to rest
Waiting to be disturbed
So they can wreak havoc on the unexpected
The blissfully ignorant
The undeserved

Persistent darkness overwhelms the mind
Blindness evades the soul
The heart cries into lost time
Smashed wishes and distant tears
Scream into the cliché of known fear
It destroys you
Sends emotions bleak
Questions your rationality and
What you truly seek

But
Even as the old and decrepit wither away
Take pride not sorrow
Hold what you love close to you
Regret no day

Inspiration derived through companionship
Is screaming out to be praised
We all end in separate time
But our ends are all the same
So make the most of it

Rip the barriers of your mind down
They are fake anyway

Have a real look
It is just an illusion
To tear us apart.

Collective Disaster

The angry clouds up above
Are detonations in the sky
With our blurry eyed vision
The clocks have stopped ticking
Belief has left, there is no religion
The science of before has forsaken us
The calendar has ended
We have done all the taking, us
We collectively destroyed humanity
We degraded and segregated those
Who we believed to possess insanity
Our experiments were wrong
We tried to play God
Curiosity caused us to reach too far
Our greed kept the knowledge advancement
We polluted our green with depressing black tar
Is this not what we asked for?
What we wanted?

The grounds shake with the familiar sounds of death
Our divisions in the world, along with the toxins
Leave us unable to take that final breath
With our laze came the birth of machine
The stars, the stripes, the fascist regime
What were we to care
When we could sit down without needing to think
Whilst others did our dirty work
Attempting our mess in a giant sink

There is no fairy tale in the end of the world
We should have been there for each other
If only we could go back in time

Do something we never mastered
Then maybe we could go back and learn
How to save this planet from this disaster

Our collective disaster.

The Lonely Ship

It used to be believed
That the horizon out in the ocean
Was the end of the world
The naked eye deceived

We set sail alone in this existence
Only to bump into others
With familiar reflections
Evident by their melancholy expressions
They too allow the forthcoming torment
With lost eyes and no resistance
Perplexed by false promises of freedom
The blinding fog allows for no perspective
It keeps us from seeing into the distance

We are held down by chains
The mind beaten, cold, the inner voice blames
The confused state of the ill thinking brain

Our division from companionship
As the lonely openness encloses
Sanctions our disturbed minds
To which it imposes
Thoughts and anxieties that should not exist
Which seem clearer then the norm
Thoughts which have escaped into the mist

The search goes on for divine intervention
Blood thirsty knowledge to satisfy our greed
There is one thing called faith
All we need to do is believe

It could end up
How the atheists wish

Dead and buried underground
Darkness invading
Light nowhere to be found

What would be the purpose?

We set sail alone
To wander our sea
We are together with one problem
In death
There is never a you and me.

.

Old Death Parts

They were old...
Strange why they would stand there
Hand in hand
Expressionless faces
Ready to go
To Fall

Why would they do it?
They had an oath
'Death do us part'
The 'part' being short
A long time together
A short time between

People would wonder
Why it was considered
And where the conversation started
They were both committing
Euthanasia
They were both committing
Suicide

They knew their end was near
They jumped together
Lost youth felt free as the wind rose
They picked up speed
Until they hit the end
At the same time
And died
With lost happiness
Sadly ever after.

Denied the Able Happiness

They look at me
With their amusing faces
As if I have celebrity status
They react to my look
With rejoice and happiness

They walk around
How unlucky!
Kelly pushes me in my chair
Otherwise I spin the wheels myself
Sometimes I dribble
She wipes it off my chin

I get jealous when she talks to others
So I make a nuisance of myself
To get her attention back to me
She sees my beauty
But would never love me
It's a shame really

I get the worst of it
When I am alone
A group of kids
Shouting obscenities
I recall one of them shouting
"Spastic"
I do not mind kids
They do not understand
The loneliness and restrictions of the chair
Their desperation to fit in

They followed me home once
I was rolling my way back
They grabbed the handles

Laughing
They took me somewhere

I was raced onto a train track
Wood jammed in-between the wheels
"One less retard," one said
They ran off
I did not cry
I was stronger than them

The train arrived at pace
The kids had already scattered
The cowards
So I sat and collected my last thoughts
As I looked back fondly
To a happy life
With an unfortunate ending.

Misplaced Anger

You insinuate to incinerate
Begin the unenviable process of burning
You torture, you torment, you intimidate
Just an unimportant prick in this world
You are overwhelming, self centred, pretentious
Get over yourself
Get your ego in proportion
Nothing you do is important
It is as useless as the rest of our actions
The difference is
You demand reactions
To get people to look
People to care
When nobody does

The brand strewn across your chest
Does not even begin to show success
Material clinging to your body
Is just another literal thing
In your pointless worthless life

I hope you read this
Learn what you really are
You will never leave a mark in this world
You will never go far.

Life's Bitter Endings

The cracked, bitter textures of life
And years of blinded following
Drag our unquestioning beings
Into sudden conflicts, 'private, we're going!'

We cower in fear and emotion
We cannot believe what we see
We sharpen the blades on our bayonets
When I was younger was this what I wanted to be?

We murder otherwise innocent people
Who are just defending their own
Following orders we end the lives of brothers, fathers,
uncles, husbands
Decent people for all we could have known
We are not good people, fighting in a justified war
No, we are here to impose our views, to get
Control and oil, greedy men just keep wanting more

Looking around I wonder about my children
Do they know Daddy's a murderer?
I can hear my daughter's voice screaming in my head
The pain I felt hurt her
'Why would you kill them Daddy, Why would you kill
them?'
Are the cries I hear
Back at home I am not a strong man
I am weak at the legs, surrounded by fear

The expressions of the men's lives I ended
Are at the forefront of my thoughts

The greedy men didn't care about me
I did the job I was taught

Physically I'm not captive
But mentally I'm incarcerated
I never got shot but
The wounds are in my mind

What would you do if you were me?
I'm told we have the right to think
That we are free
They falsely lead us to believe
That ending someone's life is legitimate
When following orders
Overseas.

Impaled on Emotion

Depression
The obsession
Blindly thought of oppression
Faltered but 'found'
By the profane and unprofound

Delusional calamity
Of diagnosed insanity
Impaled on emotion
Creating commotion of
Unwanted breath and
Thoughts of unwarranted death

Previously witnessed
We gaze into the distance for the answer
For the unanswerable question

Understanding
The reprimanding
Points of view

Bedazzled by
The lack of saddle
No-where to sit
Like the means of fitting in

All wrong in the brain
Feel the unnecessary pain

But try to prosper
Spot the imposter
He is not you

If only they knew the ecstatic or
Emphatic feeling of elation
The ironic cause of segregation

It is those with misunderstanding
Who are commanding what you need
So here we plead
Give us the companionship
Or leave us alone and
Allow us to bleed

In silence.

The Distressed Mind

Voices inside your head crave reaction
Taking away your sanity
Leading to unsafe distractions

Not knowingly given
Battles thrive in your inner mind

This cruel attempt harms your own
Causes obvious resent

Divinity is hinted
It's tinted and blinded

A haze covers the fear

Help is needed to protest what is dealt
Maybe an understanding?

Cannot blame the unfair
'It can happen to anyone' is what is said
The voices in your head
"You're a freak, a psychopath"

Everyone has their problems
Some are just more accepted than others
But that's life
And lack of peoples understanding

Leaves you alone to ask

Can someone pull you out?
At some point yes

But until then
The minds delusions
Will keep you alone.

The Mind Cycle

The cycle continues...

You start with the lows
Ultimately collaborated with mania
Let's let someone else know
What it is like to deal with insanity
Hello humanity
Here is your lesson

Let's start with the top
The ridiculous feeling of high
Adrenaline maximising your optimism
Quickly skipping between subjects
You are subjective to insults
You are victimised

Now with the bottom
The pit where you continue to fall
Lay down for an hour or two
Feel the pinnacle of worthlessness
The ever swinging pendulum
Through the extremities of moods

Affect those around you
Smear tears over their clothes
Have them be uplifting
But not understanding
For it was not you who chose this

The best are those who tell you to snap out of it
Like it's a phase that can be helped
'Stop moping around'
'Well start coping, I'm fucking down'

Go to a therapist
They will make it better
They 'get it'
Professionalism is helpful
But experience is essential
They use their text books
But do they know?
One way to find out

Great, drug prescription
Only a few side effects
At least it takes it out of the head
Momentarily
Until you realise it affects physical health
Back to therapy

At least there is someone to talk to
Pointless it may be
Bring up the sightings
The brains delusions
Realise that you are back to square one
I thought you started with the lows?

The cycle continues.

He Thought Thoughts He Thought Would Change the World

I started with fire
Then I played with ice
I managed to merge them
Into a new mystifying element
I added electricity
To give it power

That is why I am in contention
As it was my invention
Which sparked the known world

At first the people were not keen enough
But I let them see my genius
As I created something new

They were scared of change
Their frightened state left them
As I made them change
They praise me with food
And keep me warm in this nice jacket
The walls are nice and soft
I get to play on my own all day
Whilst I think about another invention

I love my new home
A good friend said I was like unsliced pie
And was going to be sectioned
That was the best day of my life
Because

I love pie
...

New Religious Movement

This is not hypnotism
Or a baptism of fire
It's fuelling the desire
Of the hidden mind
The 'id'

I shall elaborate
On my flawless beliefs
And this beautiful religion
How could you resist such promise?

Undivided attention please
I will look at a remote
And find the most suitable program for you
There are the stages of enlightenment
Do you remember there are five?

Sign the paper
It can be explained later
This slip needs a signature
The bureaucracy needs your pen-print
And the leader must make his decision

All you need to do
Is to thank the great Ken
And read his book
It's called 'Je-sussed'
Admire his prestige
But never be jealous

Well done!
We knew you could do it
You will never regret your decision
To sign

May the leader
Bring you infinite days of happiness

Big day for you
First one here!
Congratulations
You aren't going to hell
Even though it doesn't exist

Glad you are positive
Also unsurprised
That leader granted us this fine day
That's forty kenlar's please
For the blessing of sunshine

What?
You have no money?
Leader shall not be pleased
How will you fund
Your lessons?

Looks like
Your time here may be up
By mutual decision
We have done all we can to help
May you go in peace

Exit?
Sounds too much like exploitation
There's a place where people like you go
It's over there in that field
Stand on the 'X'

Your temple may feel a slight pierce
But after that you will feel nothing
All you will see is black
The colour of enlightenment

No need to thank me
Thank the leader
The Great Ken
He wishes you
A safe
And short journey
To the beginning
Of the end.

Dead Long Queue

The queue was long and wavy
The front hidden by mist
Cries of our boy wondering
What he did to deserve this

I suppose it was only a queue
Our boy just needed to learn patience
Screaming ambulances passed
Scenes not fit for this boy's innocence

As our boy edged ever closer to the end
Nervous anticipation invaded his being
He wondered about the perks
Of his upcoming fleeing

There was not long to go
His face lit up as his heart sank
The apathetic feeling
Of knowing the end was blank

When he reached the end of the queue
This boy jumped for joy and pride
Another waste of life
As this boy queued for suicide.

The Real Valentine

Sarcastic irony
Lays within false holidays
Songs are played with wretched keys
Even the deaf can't escape
Pleasure, ambition and desire
Are shoved down throats
Before the mouth gets covered with tape
A burning reflex to rid of what you hate
Is made impossible by the forced silence
The choice is not yours
Go out and buy and pay
Make the greedy, grabbing, stealing, narcissists days
The horizon is blinded, thicker than haze
You cannot find the words
A card can do it for you
Isn't that what this day is all about?

I wish to find the card for the realistic
Even those that enjoy themselves—and the ones that
hate
Can buy a 'symbol for love' and feed the sadistic
A false smile and an excuse are made for generic
gestures
Which are available throughout the whole year
So why today?

The poor and the strained relationships have a night
to fix
It is like trying to put up a house with no cement or
bricks
A false gift for the housewarming

Tomorrow will be a new day, a new life, a good
morning
But that's all it is
A morning
It won't last until the afternoon
Or the evening
And by nighttime?

Well the inevitable will approach
You will look back on these days
Thinking why you made no effort on any other
Because you are told it's the norm
Your selfishness told you not to bother

So you are not a Romeo
A romantic
You are insecure, unwilling, pedantic
Looking out for yourself
Childish antics

Work for what you have
Because before you know it
You will be in that chair
Looking out into the grey
Old and lonely
Awaiting your death
Looking back on a sad life
And how you wasted every breath
How it could have been with that one person
If you decided to make an effort
Is the curse out?
That's what I thought.

Happy Valentine's Day.

An Unnerving Description of Song

It's the creaky climb with the
Infestation of various insects
Trickling water
Invading sound waves

Light humming
Collaborates with drones
Setting alight the heavy
Brain far into the depths
Of false realities
Plunging ever further
Into the realms of insanity

Contemplating the takings
Of the precious and given
CRACK the echo deepens
WHUUUR the time rapidly rotates
Snubbing the candles which
Wait for a new member
365 days on

Wait for the chimes on the sorrowful day
Bells of forsaken truths
Clatter a ferocious mix
Rapidly getting slower
To an eventual
Standstill

It may not be over yet
The fat lady won't be around long enough
To sing the final farewell

Goodbye

Try not to hurt yourself.

The Greed in the Happiness

I hate it when things end
Except
Things never end
Never ending things

Where was the start
I wonder
Do people expect things to halt?

After placing the plate of happiness
On the oak table
By the small fire left by
The liquidised candle wax
People fight to dig in
As there is not enough to share

I wonder why
People leave the weak to crumble
Like the sadness in their apple pie
They are force fed
Hopelessness

The hungry are also cold
Lonely in a realm referred to as home
A darkness is all consuming
The light fades away
Ironically because
Shadow comes from light

A perplexing scenario
A never ending tale
Of the constant struggle
In the pursuit of happiness
That the arrogant

And ignorant
Seem freer to enjoy

I don't expect favours
I don't expect understanding

I expect when you die
You will understand
Because
You will die alone
Like the rest of us.

Imagine the Space

Go back to your world, I have a thought for you...

Think about yourself, your existence, your appearance, friends, family, associates, co-workers, acquaintances, people around you, on the street, walking, riding bikes, driving cars. Try and imagine all of their lives, their existence, their appearance, their friends, their associates, co-workers, acquaintances, people around them, on the street, walking, riding bikes, driving cars. Now imagine you are standing outside your place of residence and that you are looking at the top of your head.

Now slowly start to zoom out.

After you see your head, see your house. Keep going, see the houses on your street. Zoom out further until you can see your town and all the people busily rushing around it in a fused panic. Go further, see your county, imagine the night lights as you zoom out further to see your country, your continent, our planet. Admire the beauty of our planet and all of its attractions, pan around Earth whilst imaging the six and a half billion people that inhabit it. Think of the plants, animals, insects, waves, buildings, rocks, molecules, particles. Zoom out further, admire the solar system. Think of Mercury, Venus, Earth, Mars, Jupiter, Saturn, Uranus, Neptune and even the non planet Pluto. Keep going, imagine yourself looking at the billions of stars in the universe, spin around, look at everything around you.

Now snap back into normal life.

Think about how insignificant you are.

Work and bleed and sleep and pray and eat and shit and shave and love and hate...

'As all luck ran out, hopelessness showered down. A hand which previously nurtured flattened the skull into perplexity. Standing tall and sinking with no resistance whilst staring soberly at bleakness from a distance, the eradication of his being was contemplated. Sombre attire seemed essential, as it was consequential for his lonely state. The clouds closed in. Black was all encompassing. His posture changed as he slumped towards the ground. Tears were not shed. Crashing down a desolate mountain, he caved into eternal sleeplessness without a wooden bed. Thoughts left behind were mere residue, his consciousness met its end...

...Death was eventual, death is inevitable.'

Made in United States
Orlando, FL
12 February 2024

43625915R00067